CENGAGE Learning

Drama for Students, Volume 19

Project Editor: Anne Marie Hacht

Editorial: Michelle Kazensky, Ira Mark Milne, Jennifer Smith **Rights Acquisition and Management**: Lori Hines, Sheila Spencer, Ann Taylor **Manufacturing**: Rhonda Williams

Imaging and Multimedia: Lezlie Light, Mike Logusz, Kelly A. Quin **Product Design**: Pamela A. E. Galbreath

© 2004 by Gale. Gale is an imprint of The Gale Group, Inc., a division of Thomson Learning Inc.

Gale and Design® and Thomson Learning™ are trademarks used herein under license.

For more information, contact
Gale
27500 Drake Rd.
Farmington Hills, MI 48331-3535
Or you can visit our Internet site at

http://www.gale.com

ALL RIGHTS RESERVED
No part of this work covered by the copyright hereon may be reproduced or used in any form or by any means—graphic, electronic, or mechanical, including photocopying, recording, taping, Web distribution, or information storage retrieval systems—without the written permission of the publisher.

For permission to use material from this product, submit your request via Web at http://www.gale-edit.com/permissions, or you may download our Permissions Request form and submit your request by fax or mail to: *Permissions Department*
Gale, Inc.
27500 Drake Rd.
Farmington Hills, MI 48331-3535
Permissions Hotline:
248-699-8006 or 800-877-4253, ext. 8006
Fax: 248-699-8074 or 800-762-4058

Since this page cannot legibly accommodate all copyright notices, the acknowledgments constitute an extension of the copyright notice.

While every effort has been made to ensure the reliability of the information presented in this publication, The Gale Group, Inc. does not guarantee the accuracy of the data contained herein. The Gale Group, Inc. accepts no payment for listing; and inclusion in the publication of any organization, agency, institution, publication, service, or individual does not imply endorsement of the editors or publisher. Errors brought to the attention of the publisher and verified to the satisfaction of the publisher will be corrected in future editions.

ISBN 0-7876-68168
ISSN 1094-9232

Printed in the United States of America
10 9 8 7 6 5 4 3 2 1

Sweeney Todd: The Demon Barber of Fleet Street

Hugh Wheeler 1979

Introduction

The story of *Sweeney Todd: The Demon Barber of Fleet Street* first appeared in the 1830s in England and was soon adapted for the London stage. When Stephen Sondheim, the celebrated producer of hit Broadway musicals, saw a version of the play in London in the mid 1970s, he asked Hugh Wheeler to collaborate with him on a musical adaptation.

When the new *Sweeney Todd* opened on Broadway in 1979, it became an instant hit and later walked away with that year's Tony award—Broadway's highest honor.

The public was shocked but thoroughly entertained by the gruesome storyline of this musical thriller, which focuses on the murderous machinations of a vengeful English barber and his accommodating landlady. The play follows the barber, Sweeney Todd, as he plots his revenge against Judge Turpin, who sent him to prison on false charges—an act which causes the destruction of Sweeney's family. As Sweeney's revenge plot accidentally broadens to include other citizens of the corrupt society of Victorian London, his landlady, Mrs. Lovett, finds a way to cover up the barber's crimes as well as her own. Through this darkly comic story, Wheeler explores the motivations for, and consequences of, revenge.

Author Biography

Hugh Callingham Wheeler was born on March 19, 1912, in London, England to Harold and Florence (Scammell) Wheeler. He received a bachelor's degree in English from the University of London in 1932. Ten years later, in 1942, he became a naturalized American citizen. Wheeler's writing career began with detective novels published under three different pseudonyms: Patrick Quentin, Q. Patrick, and Jonathan Stagge. Wheeler collaborated on several of these novels with Richard Wilson Webb until 1952. *A Puzzle for Fools* (1936), written under the pen name Patrick Quentin, became the first volume in Simon and Schuster's "Inner Sanctum" mystery series and was well received.

In 1961, Wheeler found success in the theater with productions of two of his plays. *Big Fish, Little Fish*, Wheeler's first play, was produced by Sir John Gielgud and starred Jason Robards Jr. Howard Taubman, who reviewed the play for the *New York Times,* praised its "current of honest feeling and human warmth" and felt that Wheeler had written it with "beguiling integrity." Wheeler's second play *Look: We've Come Through!* was produced by Jose Quintero.

Wheeler followed these plays with the popular hit *A Little Night Music* in 1973 and *Sweeney Todd* in 1979. From the beginning, Wheeler received many awards, including several Antoinette Perry

"Tony" Awards. His first Tony was in 1973 for *A Little Night Music*, followed by one for *Candide* in 1974, and another in 1979 for *Sweeney Todd*. In 1973, Wheeler also received four Drama Critics Circle Awards for *A Little Night Music*, *Candide*, *Pacific Overtures* (written with John Weidmann), and for *Sweeney Todd*. Wheeler died of heart and lung disease on July 26, 1987, in Pittsfield, Massachusetts.

Plot Summary

Act 1

The play opens on a street by the London docks where Sweeney Todd and Anthony Hope have just come into port. When Anthony expresses his pleasure at being back in England, "the best place in the world," Sweeney suggests that he will soon be disappointed. A Beggar Woman appears and Anthony gives her money. After she tells Sweeney that he looks familiar, he shoos her away but not before she propositions him. Sweeney tells Anthony a tale of a "foolish" barber and his beautiful wife whose lives were destroyed by "a pious vulture of the law." He admits that he does not know the lady's fate.

Sweeney walks up to a pie shop on Fleet Street run by Mrs. Lovett, who admits, as she flicks flies and dirt off her pies, that the pies are "the worst" in London. She admires the "enterprising" nature of the woman down the road who bakes cats into her pies. When Sweeney asks to rent out the flat above her shop, she warns him that it is haunted by Benjamin Barker, a barber who was sent to prison by Judge Turpin and his Beadle who lusted after the barber's beautiful wife. Mrs. Lovett reveals that the wife, who was left with their year-old child, was lured to the judges' house where he raped her.

Mrs. Lovett soon recognizes that Sweeney is

the barber and tells him that after his wife Lucy poisoned herself, Judge Turpin adopted Johanna. Sweeney declares that for the fifteen years he has spent in prison "on a trumped up charge" he has been dreaming of returning to his wife and child, but now he is bent on revenge. Mrs. Lovett takes pity on him, insisting that he set up his barber shop there again and returns his silver handled razors that she has kept for all these years. Sweeney looks lovingly at his "lucky friends."

At Judge Turpin's mansion, Johanna admires a bird seller's collection as Anthony walks by, stunned by her beauty. The old Beggar Woman emerges from a pile of trash and again asks Anthony for money as she gestures lewdly. She identifies Johanna before she departs. Just as Johanna is about to take the bird Anthony has bought for her, Judge Turpin appears, followed by the Beadle, and demands that Johanna go in the house. He threatens Anthony, which is reinforced by the Beadle, who grabs the cage and breaks the bird's neck. Undaunted, Anthony determines to "steal" her.

At St. Dunstan's Marketplace, "Signor Adolfo Pirelli, Haircutter-Barber-Toothpuller to His Royal Majesty the King of Naples" sells "miracle" hair tonic, guaranteed to quickly restore a full head of hair. Tobias, Pirelli's adolescent, simple-minded assistant, hawks the elixir to the crowd. An enthusiastic audience soon begins to snatch up the bottles until Sweeney appears, declaring that the tonic smells like "piss." The crowd quickly turns into a mob, demanding that their money be returned.

Sweeney challenges Pirelli to a contest, insisting that he can shave and pull teeth with much more dexterity, betting him five pounds. As the crowd cheers, Pirelli takes up the challenge. Sweeney soon proves himself to be the superior barber and dentist, and so the Beadle declares him the victor. After the Beadle declares that Sweeney looks familiar, the barber calmly invites him over for a free shave, "the closest he will ever know."

The scene shifts to Judge Turpin's home, where he rebukes himself for his lustful thoughts of Johanna. After his desire reaches its climax, he determines that he will marry her in a few days. Entering her room, he tells her of his intentions, and she staggers back in shock.

Soon after Mrs. Lovett shoos off the Beggar Woman, Anthony appears and confesses his love for Johanna. He hatches a plan to rescue her from the "monstrous tyrant" with Sweeney's help. As Mrs. Lovett suggests that Sweeney kill Anthony so that she and the barber can raise Johanna, Pirelli arrives, asking to speak to Sweeney in private. After Pirelli demands the return of his five pounds, he admits that he knows Sweeney's true identity. Sweeney strangles the blackmailer and stuffs him in a chest. When Tobias appears, asking for Pirelli, Sweeney insists that he has left, luring Tobias downstairs with Mrs. Lovett's pies and gin.

After Judge Turpin condemns a young boy to

death, he informs the Beadle of his plans to marry Johanna. The Beadle tells him that he should neaten himself up before the wedding at a fine barber shop that he knows on Fleet Street. At the mansion, Johanna and Anthony declare their love for each other and plan to escape.

Mrs. Lovett is shocked when she discovers Pirelli's body, but Sweeney convinces her that he had no option. She quickly recovers when she spots Pirelli's purse. Judge Turpin soon arrives, and Sweeney prepares to "shave" him. The two discuss the pleasures of "pretty women" until, just as Sweeney is about to cut his throat, Anthony bursts in announcing his plans for elopement. Enraged, Judge Turpin leaves, determined to lock Johanna away. Sweeney's missed opportunity pushes him over the edge, and he begins to rant about all the people who deserve to die. As he swears vengeance, he decides that he will "practice on less honorable throats" in the meantime—the thought of which fills him with joy. Mrs. Lovett calls his attention to Pirelli's body, demanding that something be done about it. Soon though, she hatches a plan to bake him, and the others who will follow, into pies. The act closes with the two happily contemplating the justice of "those above" serving "those down below."

Act 2

Mrs. Lovett has now become a prosperous shopkeeper, thanks to the popularity of her delicious pies while Tobias waits the full tables in her shop. Sweeney has ordered a new barber chair that he attaches to a chute into the basement, his "customers" last stop before the oven. In another part of the city Anthony searches the streets for Johanna, who has been sent to an insane asylum by Judge Turpin in order to keep her away from Anthony. That evening, the old Beggar Woman sees the thick, noxious smoke billowing from the bakehouse chimney and yells, "city on fire ... smoke that comes from the mouth of hell."

The next day, as Anthony renews his search, he hears Johanna's voice coming out of a window of Fogg's Asylum for the Mentally Deranged. As he bangs on the door demanding admittance, the Beadle walks by and recognizes him. Anthony tells him that Johanna is incarcerated within by "a monstrous perversion of justice." The Beadle responds that Johanna is "mad as the seven seas" and that he brought her there himself. When Anthony refuses to leave, the Beadle whistles for the police, and Anthony runs off.

Back at the pie shop, Mrs. Lovett tries to romance Sweeney, suggesting that they find a house for the two of them by the sea. Sweeney feigns an interest he clearly does not feel, but soon returns to his obsessive quest to punish Judge Turpin. Anthony suddenly bursts in informing Sweeney that he has found Johanna. Sweeney hatches a plot to get her out, suggesting that Anthony go to the asylum posing as a wigmaker looking for a particular color of hair, which will match Johanna's. Sweeney tells

Anthony to bring her back to the shop where he will protect her while Anthony makes arrangements to escape the city.

After Anthony leaves, Sweeney writes a letter to Judge Turpin, informing him that Anthony will be bringing Johanna to the shop that evening. Downstairs, Tobias suggests that he knows there have been "evil deeds" committed and that he will protect Mrs. Lovett. When he discovers Pirelli's money purse, he is convinced that Sweeney killed his old employer in a robbery attempt. Mrs. Lovett lures Tobias into the bakehouse under the pretense of teaching him how to make pies and locks him in.

The Beadle arrives at the shop and tells Mrs. Lovett that neighbors have made complaints about the smell coming from the bakehouse chimney and that he would like to take a look. An agitated Mrs. Lovett tries to divert him, insisting that only Sweeney has the key, and he will not be back for hours. As the Beadle settles down to wait, Sweeney appears and convinces him to come upstairs for a shave. Down in the bakehouse, Tobias eats pies until he sees the Beadle's bloody body sliding down the chute. Screaming in terror, he runs to the door and realizes that he is locked in.

Anthony goes to the asylum, disguised as a wigmaker and tries to free Johanna. When confronted by Fogg, however, Anthony drops the gun he had been carrying, unable to shoot the man. Johanna finds the courage to pick up the gun and kill Fogg, and the two escape, along with the other inmates. Anthony brings Johanna, who has disguised herself as a sailor, to the barber shop. When she hears the Beggar Woman calling for the Beadle, whom she saw enter the shop, Johanna hides in the chest. The Beggar Woman, followed by Sweeney, comes up to the barber shop, insisting that there is evil there and noting that he looks familiar to her.

Sweeney, seeing Judge Turpin approach, declares that he has no time to deal with the Beggar Woman, slits her throat, and sends her body down the chute. When Judge Turpin arrives looking for Johanna, Sweeney convinces him to first get a shave. Just as Judge Turpin recognizes Sweeney, the barber cuts his throat and sends him down the chute. The commotion brings Johanna out of the chest, but Sweeney does not recognize his daughter. He lunges at her, but she escapes, while Mrs. Lovett fights off the half-dead Judge until he finally succumbs.

As Sweeney tries to stuff the Beggar Woman's body into the oven, Mrs. Lovett insists that he not touch her, admitting that the woman is Lucy, Sweeney's wife. When Sweeney realizes that Mrs. Lovett has lied to him, he pushes her into the oven, and cradles his dead wife in his arms. When Tobias emerges from a corner and sees the carnage, he picks up his razor and kills Sweeney. The play ends as Tobias turns to the grinding machine and the police arrive with Anthony and Johanna.

Characters

The Beadle

The Beadle's character is a carbon copy of Judge Turpin. He, however, has less power than Judge Turpin, and so must carry out the crimes against others, which he does with great relish. His brutality emerges as he breaks the neck of the bird that Anthony has bought for Johanna.

Beggar Woman

Sweeney does not discover that the desperate and miserable Beggar Woman is his wife, Lucy Todd, until after he has killed her. She appears throughout the play, initially as the illustration of what poor, destitute women in Victorian London were often reduced to. After Sweeney refuses her pleas for money, she lewdly propositions him. Later, she becomes the harbinger of doom as she haunts the street in front of the pie shop, trying to draw attention to the "stink of evil" within.

Anthony Hope

As his name suggests, throughout the play, Anthony is a cheerful, optimistic, country born young ship's first mate. He is a loyal friend to Sweeney, whom he courageously saved from drowning. In his determination to save the woman he loves, he faces threats from Judge Turpin and the Beadle, which include incarceration. His innocence emerges, however, when he is unable to shoot Mr. Fogg.

Mrs. Lovett

Mrs. Lovett is a vigorous, middle-aged woman who knows how to survive amidst the miserable conditions in Victorian London when "times is hard." She falls in love with Sweeney and will do anything to keep him, even cover up his crimes. This apparently is not a difficult task for her, since she profits greatly from her pies as she reveals her practicality as well as her greed. She shows a more tender side in her relationship with the Beggar Woman. Although her love for Sweeney prevents her from telling him the woman's true identity, she will allow no harm to come to Lucy and is truly despondent when she realizes that Sweeney has killed her.

Mr. Pirelli

An "excessively flamboyant Italian with a glittering suit and a dazzling smile," Mr. Pirelli becomes another example of the rampant corruption in the city. He swindles others out of their money by hawking magic elixirs that will cure all ills. After Sweeney bests him during a barbering contest, Mr. Pirelli reveals his penchant for blackmail when he threatens to reveal the barber's true identity.

Tobias Ragg

Tobias is a loyal servant, first to Pirelli and later to Mrs. Lovett, to whom he attaches like a child. He swears to protect her against the "evils" of the house, but when he fails, he takes revenge and kills Sweeney.

Johanna Todd

Johanna is the personification of innocence, at least until she is driven by circumstance to kill Mr. Fogg, the proprietor of the insane asylum to which Judge Turpin has sent her. Her love for Anthony and his for her offer the only hint of salvation in the play.

Lucy Todd

See Beggar Woman

Sweeney Todd

A saturnine, middle-aged man, the brooding Sweeney exhibits "nerve-chilling self-absorption." An extreme opposite to the innocent Anthony, the world-weary Sweeney points out the realities of Victorian London to his young friend. When Anthony expresses his pleasure at being back in England, "the best place in the world," Sweeney responds, "you are young and life has been kind to you. You will learn." Sweeney neither trusts nor believes in anyone except Anthony as he expresses in his response to Anthony's insistence that any good Christian would have helped save a fellow sailor. Sweeney disagrees, insisting many Christians would have turned their back on him and "not lost a wink's sleep for it, either."

His quest to avenge the breakup of his family becomes obsessive until he becomes as corrupt as the city he rails against. Blackmail and his fear that Pirelli will expose him initiate his murderous turn. He soon gains a lust, though, for murder as he "practices on less honorable throats" while he awaits Judge Turpin's visit to his barbershop. By the end of the play, he has become insane after killing his wife and Mrs. Lovett.

Media Adaptations

- *Sweeney Todd* was produced for television in a 1998 production, directed by John Schlesinger and starring Ben Kingsley as Sweeney.

- A filming of a live stage performance was shown on television in 2001, starring George Hearn and Patti LuPone. This version is now available in video and DVD formats.

Judge Turpin

Along with the Beadle, Judge Turpin is the personification of evil and corruption. His lechery toward Lucy, and later toward Johanna, inspires his treachery, which causes the destruction of Sweeney's family. His amoral nature allows no conscience as he has Sweeney deported to Australia under false charges and as he lures the despondent Lucy to his mansion where he rapes her.

Mrs. Lovett determines that he must have "a conscience tucked away" when he adopts Johanna in a seemingly altruistic move. However, his harsh treatment of her reveals his true motive—his lecherous intentions toward the beautiful young girl. Even as he whips himself in punishment for his desire for her, calling out to God to forgive him and restrain him, his lust drives him into a frenzy that, when abated, makes him determined to take her against her will into marriage. When Anthony threatens Judge Turpin's control over Johanna, he shows no mercy as he abandons her in an insane asylum. His lack of mercy, along with his hypocrisy, is applied universally when he passes a death sentence out to a young boy who comes before him in court.

Themes

Corruption

The play's focus on corruption is announced by Sweeney in the first scene when he describes London as "a great black pit" inhabited by "the vermin of the world." There is no morality in Sweeney's London where "at the top of the hole *Sit the privileged few* Turning beauty into filth and greed." Judge Turpin becomes an illustration of one of those privileged few whose "justice" is meted out according to his own greedy appetites. He sends Sweeney off to a prison colony in Australia on false charges so that Judge Turpin can more easily lure Sweeney's wife into his bed. Turpin's hypocrisy emerges in his treatment of a young boy who comes before his court. Insisting that it is his "earnest wish ever to temper justice with mercy," he nevertheless determines that he cannot be lenient to someone who repeatedly commits crimes. Thus, he sentences the boy to death as he plots to coerce his charge, Johanna, into marriage so that he can satisfy his lust for her.

The play also illustrates how the lower classes are forced into similar states of corruption in a system that allows them little dignity. The horrendous realities of poverty in Victorian London, which offered no social safety nets, help promote blackmail and murder as individuals struggle for survival. Mr. Pirelli resorts to the former when Sweeney threatens his livelihood by besting him in a barbering contest. Sweeney and Mrs. Lovett turn to murder, prompted by revenge and greed. Neither sees any other direction for their dismal lives. Sweeney becomes obsessed with righting the wrong that was done to his family, while Mrs. Lovett collaborates with him so that she can sell enough pies to keep a roof over her head.

Loss of Innocence

The rampant corruption in the city causes the characters to lose their innocence. Sweeney admits that he was "foolish" in his initial belief that he and his wife, who was "his reason and his life," could find happiness together. He is soon forced to face reality when Judge Turpin, "a pious vulture of the law," destroys their family. Sweeney has now become a world-weary cynic who tells Anthony, whose own innocence prompts him to declare that London is the best place in the world, "You are young. Life has been kind to you. You will learn."

Lucy, Sweeney's wife, has experienced a more devastating loss of innocence after her husband is sent to prison. Judge Turpin, who rapes her, and the system, which allows no opportunities for a fallen woman, have corrupted the once beautiful and virtuous woman. In order to survive, she must beg for money and prostitute herself on the streets of London.

Topics for Further Study

- Think about how a dramatic version of *Sweeney Todd* could be produced without the musical passages. Determine what scenes or dialogue you would have to add if you cut out these passages.
- Research the original version of *Sweeney Todd* written by George Dibden-Pitt and trace the development of the story into Wheeler's play.
- Read Jonathan Swift's satire "A Modest Proposal," which also focuses on cannibalism. Compare and contrast it to the play.
- Investigate the living conditions of the lower class in Victorian London. Does the play present a realistic

depiction of these conditions?

One of the focal points of the play is Anthony and Sweeney's efforts to ensure that Judge Turpin does not take Johanna's innocence as he did her mother's. Anthony is able to eventually save Johanna's virtue but not before she is exposed to the harsh realities of indigent Londoners who are confined to mental asylums. Her experience there, coupled with Judge Turpin's treatment of her, hardens her to the point that she is able to shoot the proprietor of the asylum in order to make her escape.

Revenge

The overwhelming corruption along with the loss of innocence Sweeney experiences creates an obsession for revenge. Initially, his goal is only to kill Judge Turpin and the Beadle in payment for their crimes against his family, but when Pirelli threatens to thwart his plans, Sweeney embarks on a murder spree that widens his revenge scheme to include social as well as personal retribution. Aided by Mrs. Lovett, who acts purely on greed, Sweeney determines that "the history of the world ... is who gets eaten and who gets to eat." Thus, he will "practice on less honorable throats," shifting the balance of social power to the lower classes, until he has a chance to exact his revenge on Judge Turpin. Sweeney's obsessive quest, however, pushes him over the edge of sanity and ultimately destroys him.

Style

Musical

More than half of the play is sung, often without a clear melody, and employs natural, conversational syntax. The play opens with a prologue sung by the company that outlines its main focus. The musical sequences that follow often provide symbolic echoes of the plot. For example, in the first scene after Sweeney and Anthony arrive in London, Anthony sings the city's praises. Sweeney has a contrary view of London, however, that he expresses in a song which describes the city as "a hole in the world; *Like a great black pit* And the vermin of the world / Inhabit it." His vitriolic personification of the city reflects his anger over the loss of his wife and daughter. Ironically, he will eventually fall into that same pit of corruption.

Later Johanna sings out the window of Judge Turpin's house, feeling like the confined birds she sees the street vender hawking: "Have you decided it's / Safer in cages, *Singing when you're told?* My cage has many rooms ... *Nothing there sings,* not even my lark."

Dramatic Structure

As the plot unfolds, Wheeler often creates a collage of scenes, making quick cuts back and forth between story lines. This juxtaposition emphasizes the thematic unity in the play. One such segment involves Sweeney and Anthony. As the scene cuts back and forth between the two characters, the play's focus on the interplay of innocence and corruption is reinforced. The scene opens with Anthony searching the streets of London for Johanna, singing of her beauty and insisting that he will save her. While he continues the search in one corner of the stage, the barber shop is lit in another, where Sweeney also praises Johanna's beauty. He doubts though that he will see her again. The two men sing her name together as Sweeney vents his rage by slitting a customer's throat. An ironic touch is added when the customer's mouth opens simultaneously with theirs as his throat is cut.

Historical Context

Victorian London

The distinction between the wealthy and lower classes was quite evident in London during the nineteenth century. A small portion of the city was set aside for well-kept residences and shopping areas. Upper and middle-class residents stayed in these areas, predominantly in the West end, fearing to venture into the remaining three quarters of the city, especially in the rough East end, which was teeming with devastating poverty and corruption. The gulf between the rich and poor widened each year. New villages continually emerged, especially near the docks, but even though Londoners found work in the city's busy port, wages were not high enough to live on. The extreme stratification of the city was studied by Karl Marx. His observations on the causes, effects, and solutions to the problem of poverty in London became the inspiration for the Communist revolutions of the following century.

Melodrama

The melodrama emerged in Italy late in the sixteenth century but did not develop into a specific genre until the end of the eighteenth century in France. Early notable melodramas include Rousseau's *Pygmalion* in 1775 and Gabiot's *L'Auto-da-Fe* in 1790. The melodrama reached its height in

England in the nineteenth century, due in part to the increasing popularity of the Gothic novel. Novels by Scott, Dickens, Wilkie Collins and other popular authors were adapted into this form for British audiences.

This genre is characterized by its sensationalism and extravagant emotion and its action and violence. Characters tend to be stereotypical in melodramas, representing extremes of good and evil. The action, which was often violent, incorporated blood, storms, spectres, witches, vampires, and other elements of the supernatural, as well as more sordid, realistic details such as alcoholism, prostitution, and murder. The most notable nineteenth-century melodramas include Thomas Holcroft's *A Tale of Mystery* in 1802, Douglas Jerrold's *Black-Eyed Susan* in 1829, Tom Taylor's *The Ticket-of-Leave Man* in 1853, and Henry Arthur Jones's *The Silver King* in 1882. At the end of the century, George Bernard Shaw adopted the form for his *The Devil's Disciple* in 1897 and *Passion, Poison, and Petrification* in 1905. In *Sweeney Todd*, Wheeler and Sondheim updated this traditional form, adding musical numbers and a social consciousness.

Critical Overview

In 1830, George Dibden-Pitt penned the story of the fictitious "Sweeney Todd," which was published in a London "penny dreadful," similar to today's tabloids. Like the present day version, this story followed a mad barber who slit his customers' throats before his landlady baked them into pies. The story was well received and Dibden-Pitt soon wrote a popular stage version of the melodrama.

In 1968, British actor Christopher Bond was scheduled to appear in the play but found the show as it was written "crude, repetitive, and simplistic—hardly any plot and less character development" and so rewrote it, crossing, as he notes, Dumas's *The Count of Monte Cristo* with Tourneur's *The Revenger's Tragedy* with a bit of Shakespeare and local "market patter" thrown into the mix. Audiences approved of Bond's version, which was revived periodically until Stephen Sondheim saw it in London in the mid-1970s and asked Hugh Wheeler to write the book for a musical version.

Compare & Contrast

- **Mid-Nineteenth Century:** From 1810 to 1852 approximately 140,000 convicts are shipped to Australia from Britain. This practice ends as the complaints from other

Australians grow louder.

1979: Americans are wrestling with the question of the death penalty and early-leave programs as overcrowding in prisons continues.

Today: Americans are still wrestling with the question of the death penalty and early-leave programs as overcrowding in prisons continues.

- **Mid-Nineteenth Century:** The lower classes are pessimistic about ever rising out of poverty since there are few social programs in place to help them.

  1979: The dominant attitude in this year is also pessimism as Americans lose faith in human nature, having experienced the assassinations of John F. Kennedy, Robert Kennedy, and Martin Luther King Jr. during the previous decade.

  Today: The dominant attitude is apprehension as terrorist attacks continue around the world.

- **Mid-Nineteenth Century:** Theatres are known as "Blood Tubs," which reflect the lurid subject matter of the plays produced in them.

  1979: Theatergoers are shocked by the violence in *Sweeney Todd*.

Today: Revivals of the play still occur, with the bloody scenes intact, but most violence in the arts is saved for the cinema, which has become increasingly violent in the past few decades.

Wheeler's and Sondheim's *Sweeney Todd* first appeared on Broadway at the Uris Theatre on March 1, 1979 and became an instant hit with critics and theater-goers alike. Some reviewers, as noted by Markland Taylor in his review of a revival of the play, decided that the "vast Industrial Revolution constructivist settings overpowered its essentially intimate story." Most critics, however, praised the production. Richard Eder, in his review for *The New York Times,* wrote, "There is more of artistic energy, creative personality and plain excitement in *Sweeney Todd* than in a dozen average musicals." While he insists that the "social commentary doesn't work," Eder judges the play "an extraordinary, fascinating, and often ravishingly lovely effort."

What Do I Read Next?

- Wheeler's *A Little Night Music* (1974) also reflects the cynicism of America in the 1970s.

- Jonathan Swift's satire "A Modest Proposal" (1729) suggests a solution to the poverty and hunger in Ireland: babies should be bred and eaten.

- Richard Altick's *Victorian People and Ideas* (1973) examines "different voices of Victorian social and intellectual history."

- Sally Mitchell's *Daily Life in Victorian England* (1996) focuses on a variety of lifestyles during this period from country gentry to urban slum dwellers.

Sources

Bond, Christopher, Introduction to *Sweeney Todd: The Demon Barber of Fleet Street,* by Hugh Wheeler and Stephen Sondheim, Applause, 1979, pp. 1–9.

Eder, Richard, "Stage: Introducing *Sweeney Todd,*" in the *New York Times,* March 2, 1979, p. C3.

Fraser, Barbara Means, "The Dream Shattered: America's Seventies Musicals," in *Journal of American Culture,* Vol. 12, No. 3, Fall 1989, pp. 31–37.

Henry, William A., III, Review of *Sweeney Todd,* in *Time,* Vol. 134, No. 13, September 25, 1989, p. 76.

Hirsch, Foster, "A Little Sondheim Music (III)," in his *Harold Prince and the American Musical Theatre,* Cambridge University Press, 1989, p. 120.

Orchard, Lee F., "Stephen Sondheim and the Disintegration of the American Dream: A Study of the Work of Stephen Sondheim from *Company* to *Sunday in the Park with George,*" Ph.D. Dissertation, University of Oregon, 1988, pp. 398–99, 468.

Schlesinger, Judith, "Psychology, Evil, and *Sweeney Todd,* or 'Don't I Know You, Mister?'" in *Stephen Sondheim: A Casebook,* edited by Joanne Gordon, Garland, 1997, p. 131.

Sondheim, Stephen, "Larger than Life: Reflections

on Melodrama and Sweeney Todd," in *Melodrama,* a special edition (Vol. 7) of *New York Literary Forum,* edited by Daniel Gerould, 1980, pp. 3, 10–14.

Sondheim, Stephen, and Hugh Wheeler, *Sweeney Todd, The Demon Barber of Fleet Street,* Dodd, Mead, 1979.

Taubman, Howard, Review of *Big Fish, Little Fish,* in the *New York Times,* March 16, 1961.

———, Review of *Look: We've Come Through!,* in the *New York Times,* October 26, 1961.

Taylor, Markland, Review of *Sweeney Todd: The Demon Barber of Fleet Street,* in *Variety,* May 13–19, 1996, pp. 78–79.

Wheeler, Hugh, *Sweeney Todd: The Demon Barber of Fleet Street,* Applause Theatre Book Publishers, 1991.

> "THE FIGURES WERE ALMOST TOTEMIC IN THE ORIGINAL, GRAND GROTESQUES BY VIRTUE OF THEIR MAKE-UP AND THE PERFORMANCE OF CARIOU AND LANSBURY."

Further Reading

Adler, T. P., "Musical Dramas of Stephen Sondheim: Some Critical Approaches," in *Pop Culture,* Vol. 12, Winter 1978, pp. 513–25.

> Adler looks at various critical approaches to Sondheim's musicals, focusing on the interplay of music and drama.

Bordman, Gerald, *American Musical Theatre: A Chronicle,* Oxford University Press, 1995.

> Bordman presents a comprehensive examination of the musical from its origins to 1990.

Jones, John Bush, "From Melodrama to Tragedy: The Transformation of *Sweeney Todd,*" in *New England Theatre Journal,* Vol. 1, No. 2, 1991, pp. 85–97.

> Jones traces the development of the story of Sweeney Todd from its original version to the musical.

Schiff, Stephen, "Deconstructing Sondheim," in the *New Yorker,* Vol. 69, March 8, 1993, pp. 76–87.

> Schiff discusses Sondheim's revolutionary modernist style and themes.